WOMEN IN STEM

SUE HENDRICKSON DINOSAUR DISCOVERER

by Clara MacCarald

Pogo Books, an imprint of Jump! Library by FlutterBee

Ideas for Parents and Teachers

Pogo Books let children practice reading informational text while introducing them to nonfiction features such as headings, labels, sidebars, maps, and diagrams, as well as a table of contents, glossary, and index.

Carefully leveled text with a strong photo match offers early fluent readers the support they need to succeed.

Before Reading

- "Walk" through the book and point out the various nonfiction features. Ask the student what purpose each feature serves.
- Look at the glossary together. Read and discuss the words.

During Reading

- Have the child read the book independently.
- Invite them to list questions that arise from reading.

After Reading

- Discuss the child's questions. Talk about how they might find answers to those questions.
- Prompt the child to think more. Ask: What did you know about dinosaur fossils before reading this book? What more would you like to learn about them?

Pogo Books are published by Jump!
3500 American Blvd W, Suite 150
Bloomington, MN 55431
www.jumplibrary.com

Jump! is a division of FlutterBee Education Group.

Library of Congress Cataloging-in-Publication Data is available at www.loc.gov or upon request from the publisher.

ISBN: 979-8-89662-382-3 (hardcover)
ISBN: 979-8-89662-383-0 (paperback)
ISBN: 979-8-89662-384-7 (ebook)

Editor: Katie Chanez
Designer: Emma Almgren-Bersie

Photo Credits: Capital Pictures/Imago, cover (foreground), 12–13; Vlad G/Shutterstock, cover (*T. rex*); releon8211/iStock, 1; vicvaz/iStock, 3; JOHN ZICH/AFP/Getty, 4; EXTREME-PHOTOGRAPHER/iStock, 5; author/iStock, 6–7; GERALDO CASO/AFP/Getty, 8; ALLVISIONN/iStock, 10–11; John Weinstein/Field Museum Library/Getty, 14–15; christopherarndt/iStock, 16; Tribune Content Agency LLC/Alamy, 17; leonello/iStock, 18–19; schusterbauer/Adobe Stock, 20–21; Minakryn Ruslan/Adobe Stock, 23.

Printed in the United States of America at Corporate Graphics in North Mankato, Minnesota.

TABLE OF CONTENTS

CHAPTER 1

A LOVE OF ADVENTURE

Sue Hendrickson has always loved adventure. Sue was born in 1949. She grew up in Munster, Indiana. Even as a kid, she wanted to travel. She read books about faraway places.

As a young adult, Sue made a living by finding things. She was a scuba diver. She explored **shipwrecks**. She searched for treasure.

Millions of years ago, tree sap covered insects. Over time, the sap hardened. It turned into **amber**. The insects inside became **fossils**.

Miners dig amber out of the ground. Most amber doesn't have anything in it. Sue bought amber that had insects inside. Then she sold them to museums.

DID YOU KNOW?

Sue found three butterflies in amber. They were more than 24 million years old!

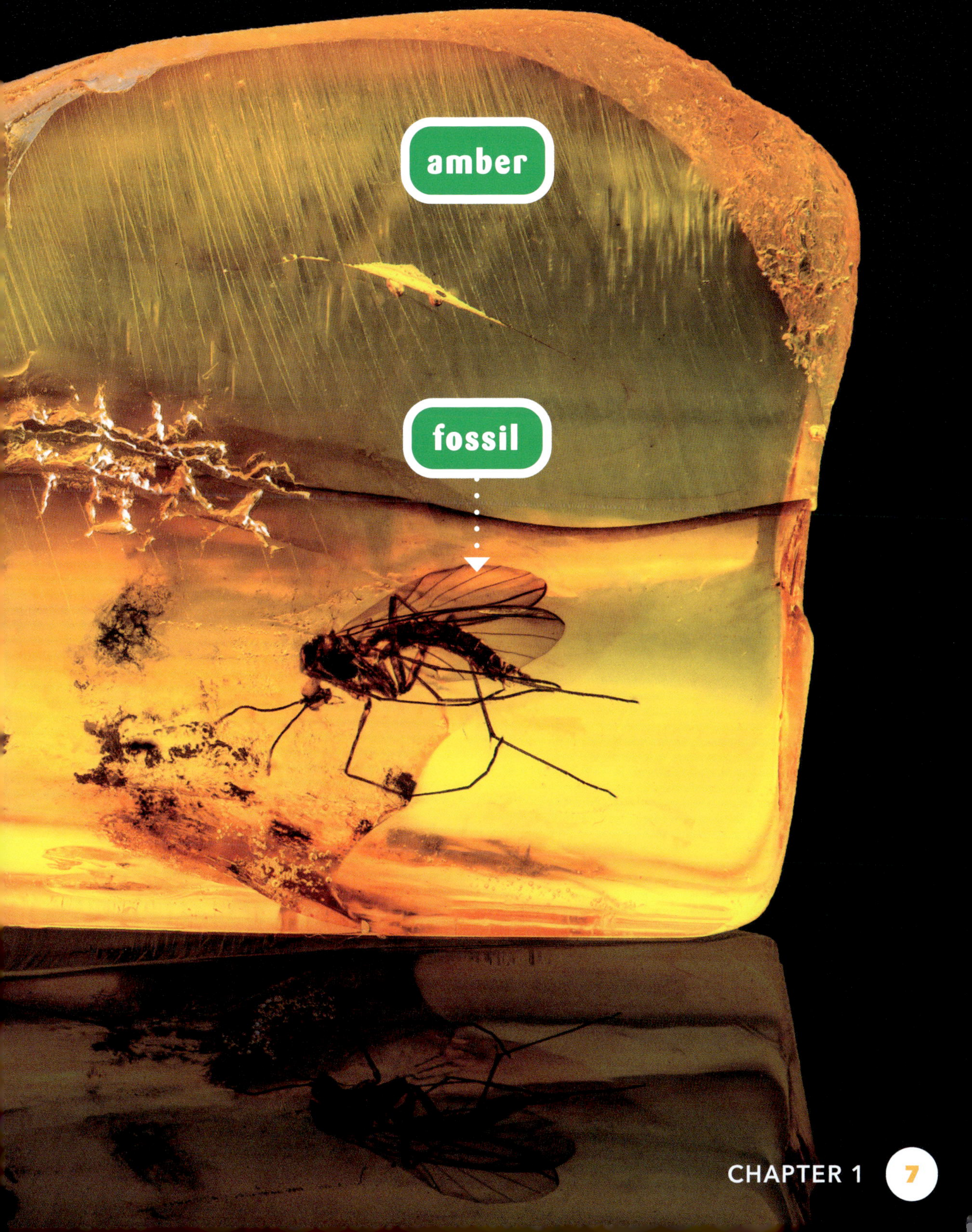
amber
fossil

CHAPTER 2

A HUGE DISCOVERY

In 1984, a scientist invited Sue to a dig. They were looking for large fossils. They traveled to Peru. They found **ancient** whale fossils. Sue helped **excavate** them.

Sue was hooked. In 1987, she joined a team that looked for dinosaur fossils. They worked near Faith, South Dakota. Rocks there date back to the time of the dinosaurs!

Dinosaurs lived more than 66 million years ago. Sometimes, when they died, mud or sand buried their bodies. Their bones became fossils. Sue and her team found many fossils. In 1990, they found a *Triceratops* **skeleton**. Parts were broken. Others were missing. Sue kept looking.

Triceratops

TAKE A LOOK!

What is one way a dinosaur fossil formed? Take a look!

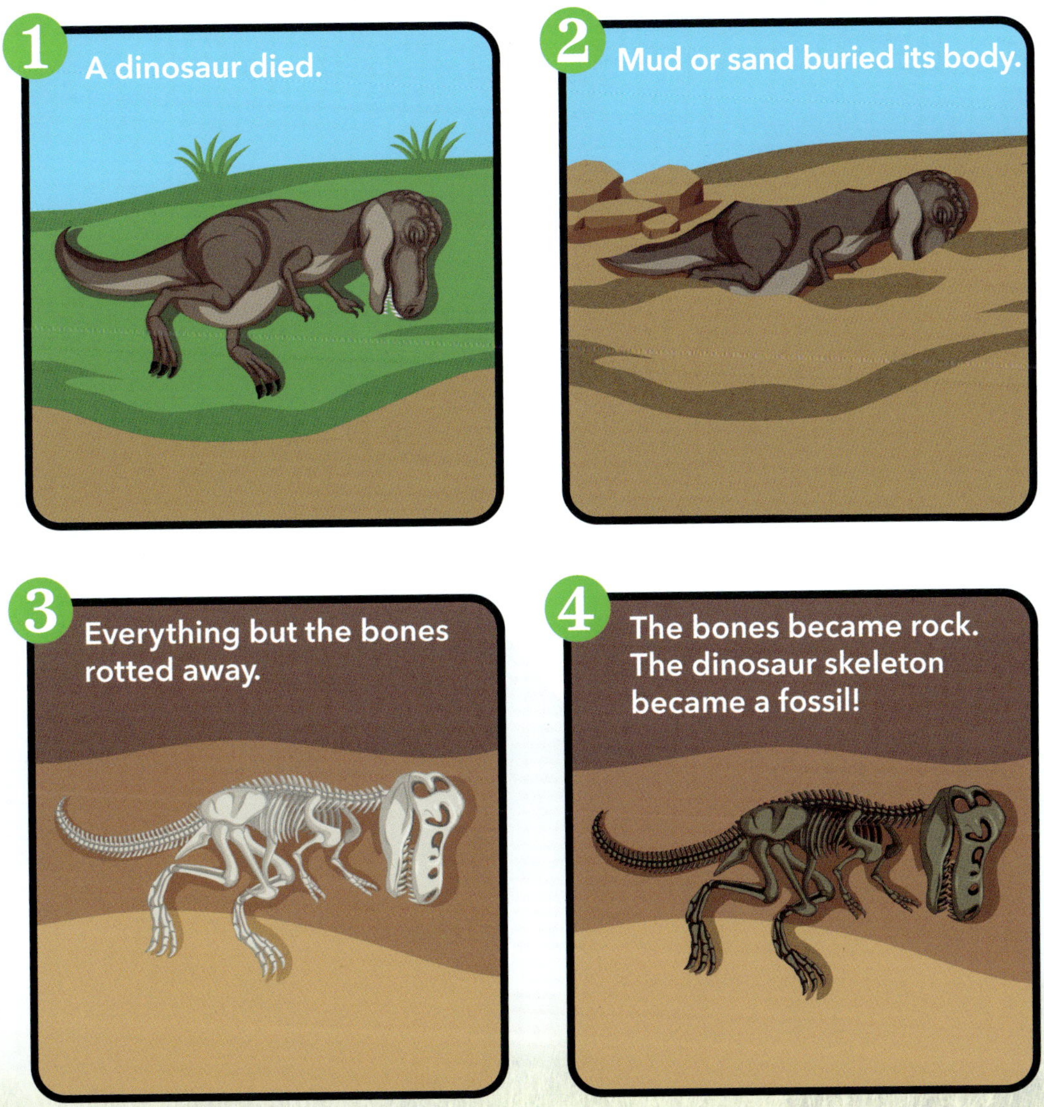

fossil

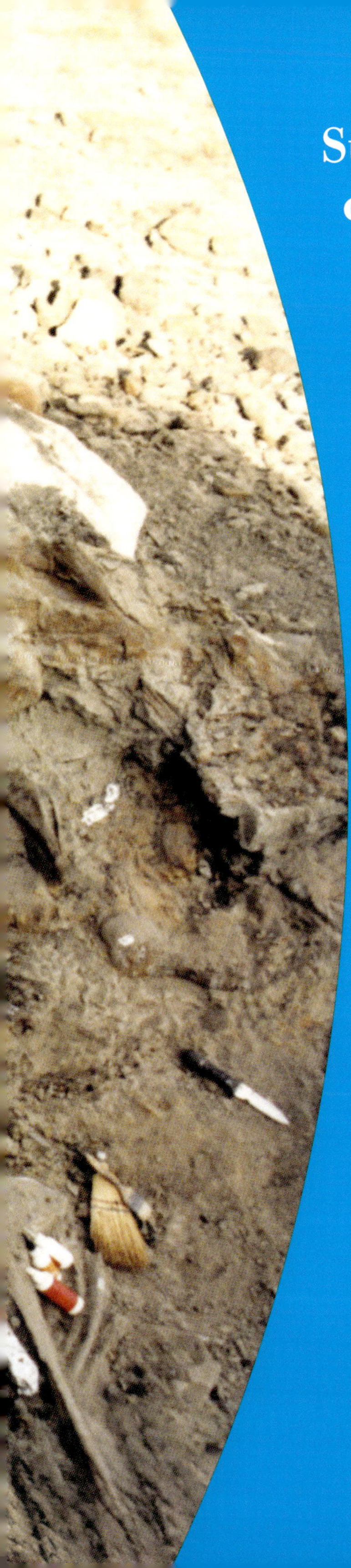

Sue saw fossils sticking out of a cliff. They were huge! Sue knew she had found something special.

The team started excavating. Digging fossils is tricky. Diggers must be careful. Why? They don't want to break the fossils.

DID YOU KNOW?

Sue and five other people excavated the fossils. They worked for 17 days!

The team brought the pieces back to a **laboratory**. The fossils belonged to a *Tyrannosaurus rex*. It was 40.5 feet (12 meters) long. It is the most complete *T. rex* skeleton ever found. It may also be the largest *T. rex* found!

CHAPTER 3

A DINOSAUR NAMED SUE

The team named the dinosaur after Sue. In 1997, SUE the *T. rex* got a new home. It went to the Field Museum of Natural History in Chicago, Illinois.

The museum put the skeleton together. Workers made fake fossils. These replaced missing ones. In 2000, SUE was ready for visitors.

Scientists have learned a lot from the skeleton. SUE died 67 million years ago. SUE was at least 28 years old. How do scientists know? Dinosaur bones formed a ring every year, like trees. They counted the rings! But there are some things scientists don't know. Like what? They don't know if SUE was male or female.

DID YOU KNOW?

Scientists have made many **casts** of SUE's fossils. They study them. The casts of SUE have gone to other museums.

In 2024, Sue visited SUE again. She was happy people could see how special SUE is.

Scientists use SUE to learn more about *T. rexes*. For example, they looked closely at SUE's skull. They found *T. rexes* had a great sense of smell! What more would you like to learn about *T. rexes*?

ACTIVITIES & TOOLS

TRY THIS!

TOY FOSSILS

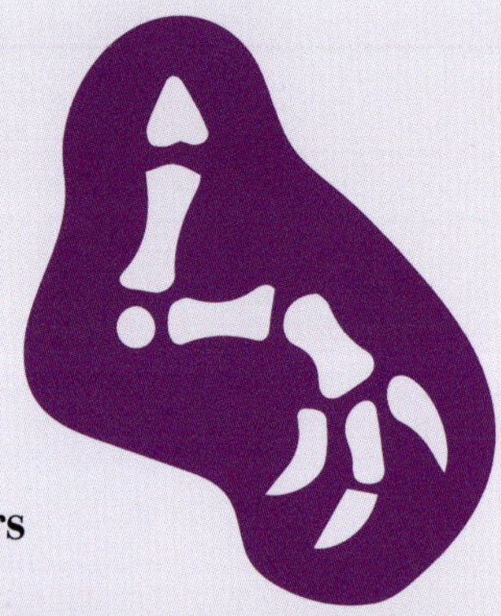

Make your own fossils with this fun activity!

What You Need:

- 2 cups (250 grams) flour
- 1 cup (273 g) salt
- ¾ cup (177 milliliters) water
- bowl
- small toy figurines, such as plastic dinosaurs
- glue

1. **Mix the flour, salt, and water in the bowl until it forms a soft dough.**
2. **Roll a handful of the dough into a ball. Flatten it into a circle.**
3. **Repeat Step 2 to make a few more flat circles of dough.**
4. **Press a toy into each flat dough circle. Lift it out. The shape of the toy should be left behind.**
5. **Pour glue into each shape.**
6. **Leave the circles somewhere safe. Let them dry for at least one day.**
7. **When the glue is dry, pull it gently out of the dough. This is your fossil!**
8. **Look at your fossil. What details do you see?**

GLOSSARY

amber: A yellow or brown fossil made of hardened tree sap.

ancient: Belonging to a period long ago.

casts: Models that are made of plaster or other materials to copy an object.

excavate: To dig something out.

fossils: Bones, shells, or other traces of animals or plants from millions of years ago preserved as rock.

laboratory: A room or building that has special equipment for people to use for scientific discoveries or experiments.

shipwrecks: The remains of sunken ships.

skeleton: A set of bones that makes up a body.

INDEX

TO LEARN MORE

Finding more information is as easy as 1, 2, 3.

1. Go to www.factsurfer.com
2. Enter "Sue Hendrickson" into the search box.
3. Choose your book to see a list of websites.

FACT SURFER